Craft it with HAMA BEADS

Easy and fun patterns for gifts and accessories from fuse beads

Prudence Rogers

David and Charles

CONTENTS

INTRODUCTION

Fuse beads have long been a popular material used for creating eye-catching and stunning objects, while allowing your imagination to run wild. Beads are arranged on a plastic pegboard and then ironed to melt them together. The brightly coloured beads are inexpensive, accessible and versatile, making them a perfect crafting medium for adults as well as kids.

It's so easy to create fun, colourful designs that, with very little equipment, can be turned into pictures, jewellery, 3d objects, gifts, home ware and much more. This book is packed with ideas for crafty creations, but don't limit yourself to what you see here – adapt, personalize and change colours wherever you want to – it's simple to add your own creativity with fuse beads. There's something extremely satisfying about watching all the tiny beads fuse and solidify to make your design permanent!

Fuse Bead Brands

There are many different brands of fuse beads available, the main ones being Hama in Europe and Perler in the US. These are both good quality and have consistent melting rates, meaning it's usually possible to mix these brands if desired without too much trouble. However, the outcome is likely to be less reliable if you use some of the cheaper beads, as their melting rates are often inconsistent and the sizes of beads tend to vary. Other popular brands include Nabbi and Pyssla (available from Ikea).

Any type of fuse beads can be used for the designs in this book, just be sure to check which sized beads are required for each project.

Warning

If you are planning on letting the kids get creative with their designs, make sure they leave the ironing to an adult to avoid injury.

USING FUSE BEADS

Buying beads

Sizes – Standard size fuse beads are 5mm in diameter and are termed Midi beads (Hama). These are the most common size of beads and are suitable from age five upwards. It's also possible to buy larger beads, which are around 10mm and although not used in this book, they are great for younger children. Finally, Mini beads (approx 2.5mm) are the smallest beads available and are suitable for 10 years and over. It's possible to get much more detail into smaller designs with these tiny beads.

Take note whether 2.5mm (Mini) or 5mm (Midi) beads are used for each project – it makes a huge difference to the size of your finished piece (see image). It's possible to use the same charts in either Mini or Midi beads, but just take note of finished sizes.

This house design can be created using either Midi or Mini beads. (See Home Sweet Home Keyring for chart)

Colours – Fuse beads come in an amazing array of colours, including solid, translucent, pastel, glitter and even glow-in-the-dark! Take a look at the website for your brand of beads and download a colour chart to see what's available. The charts in this book don't specify colour codes, as this will depend which type of beads you are using. Use colour charts to match and select the colours you need, or be inspired and choose your own.

When starting out with fuse beads, it makes sense to buy a big jar of mixed beads, as these are cheap and great for practising new ideas. However, as you try more challenging designs, such as those in this book, you will almost always end up having to sort the beads. Therefore it's much easier and quicker to buy packs of individual coloured beads.

Equipment

Besides the beads themselves, one of the great things about fuse beads is that you need very little equipment.

Pegboards – Flat plastic boards with tiny pegs that hold your beads in place while you're working them are available from many craft retailers. Different shaped boards are available, although in this book, all the charts are designed to work on the standard 29 x 29 (beads) interlocking pegboards, as they are the most versatile, allowing for any shape or size design. For the Mini fuse bead (2.5mm) designs, you will need a similar board, but with smaller pegs.

Tweezers – Although not essential, you may find it easier and quicker in some instances to use tweezers for placing beads onto the pegboard. This is particularly true for Mini fuse beads (2.5mm). Longer tweezers with pointed ends are the most useful, allowing you to pick up beads from the edges, or by grabbing the centre hole.

TIP

Some designs use the holes in the beads to create/ finish the project, so be sure to check before you go crazy with the iron and lose all your holes!

Iron and ironing paper – You will need a standard clothes iron with variable heat settings to fuse/melt the individual beads together. Smaller compact or travel irons are ideal, as they are easy to hold and control. You will need ironing paper to cover your beads to prevent melting onto the iron. Specific paper for fuse beads is available, or alternatively, use greaseproof (wax) paper.

Creating a design

To create the designs in this book, simply add the corresponding colour beads to the pegboard following the chart supplied. Each square on the chart represents one bead on the board. For larger designs, it may help if you mark off the squares on the chart as you place your beads so you can keep track of where you are.

Ironing

1 Place ironing paper over your finished design on the pegboard, ensuring all the beads are completely covered.

2 Set your iron to the required heat setting (low/ medium for Mini fuse beads 2.5mm, high for Midi fuse beads 5mm) and when it reaches the required temperature, iron the paper while keeping the iron level. Let the iron do the work – it's not necessary to apply additional pressure working evenly over the design. As the beads start to melt, they will appear darker through the paper, which means they are ready. Ensure you have ironed all the beads, paying particular attention to the edges or any areas that are only attached by one bead to make sure they are well fused.

3 Carefully peel off one edge of the paper to check that all the beads have been fused. If any beads have been missed, lay the paper back down and apply further heat to those areas. Lift the paper off to reveal the fused design.

4 Flip the pegboard over onto a heatproof surface and (optionally) repeat the process to fuse the reverse of the design (see Ironing choices).

5 After ironing, the beads will remain hot for a short while, so be careful when handling. Place a flat heavy object, such as a book, onto your design while it's cooling to ensure it remains flat (alternatively, to shape your design see Bending).

Ironing choices

You have a couple of choices when ironing designs, which really come down to personal preference of the look you favour, or what type of project is being created.

The longer the beads are ironed, the more they will spread. Eventually the hole in the centre will disappear completely. This gives a very strong finished piece, but also alters the look of the design the most. Ironing on just one side retains the look of the unfused design, while melting both sides will provide much greater strength and flexibility for crafting. For the projects in this book, unless stated otherwise, designs have been fused on both sides – just enough to melt the beads to form a good bond, but still retaining the holes. Experiment and see what you prefer!

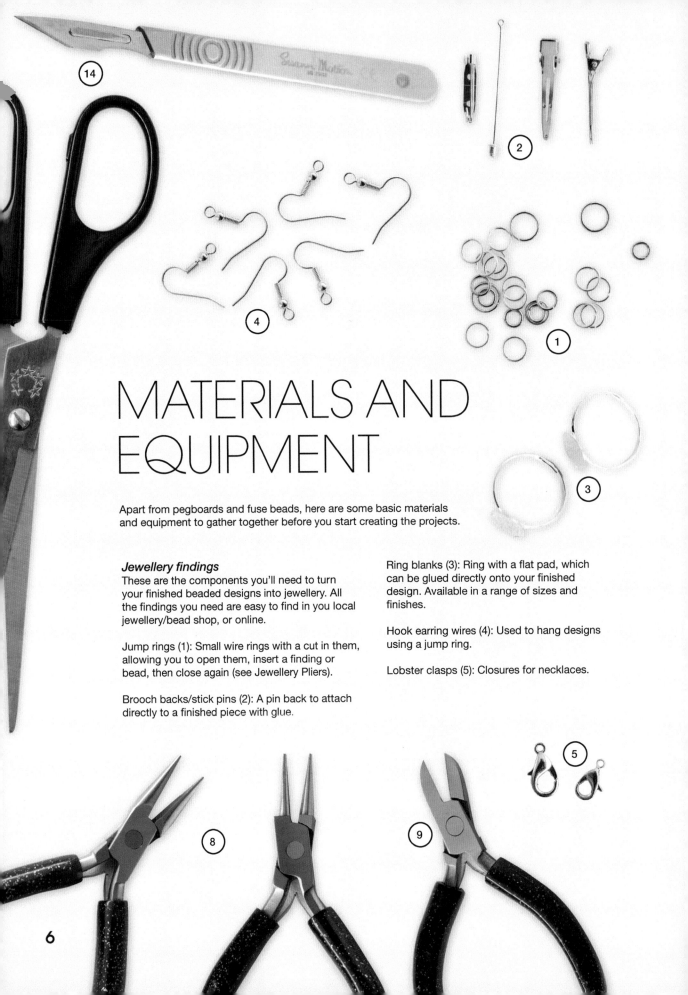

MATERIALS AND EQUIPMENT

Apart from pegboards and fuse beads, here are some basic materials and equipment to gather together before you start creating the projects.

Jewellery findings
These are the components you'll need to turn your finished beaded designs into jewellery. All the findings you need are easy to find in you local jewellery/bead shop, or online.

Jump rings (1): Small wire rings with a cut in them, allowing you to open them, insert a finding or bead, then close again (see Jewellery Pliers).

Brooch backs/stick pins (2): A pin back to attach directly to a finished piece with glue.

Ring blanks (3): Ring with a flat pad, which can be glued directly onto your finished design. Available in a range of sizes and finishes.

Hook earring wires (4): Used to hang designs using a jump ring.

Lobster clasps (5): Closures for necklaces.

Chains/necklaces

Ready-made necklaces (6): Available in a huge range of styles, colours, lengths and finishes.

Chain (7): Available to buy per metre in a range of finishes, or cut up existing necklaces with jewellery wire cutters (see Jewellery Pliers).

Jewellery pliers

These make it easy to finish of your projects with a professional look. The most useful pliers for the projects in this book are:

Chain-nose/round-nose pliers (8): Used for opening and closing jump rings, creating loops and manipulating findings.

Wire cutters (9): A pair of jewellery wire cutters will give nice clean cuts to ready-made chains and findings.

Cords, Ribbon and Needle

Beading thread (10): A firm, twisted cord for threading beads. Available in different thicknesses and a huge array of colours.

Stretch elastic thread (11): Strong, elastic cord for jewellery making, available in several different colours and thicknesses.

Ribbon (12): Used to embellish finished designs.

Embroidery thread (13): Multi-strand threads for sewing/embellishing.

Darning needle: Blunt-ended needle used for bead weaving.

Scissors/craft knife (14): Used for cutting templates, ribbon, thread etc. and trimming fused beads.

Glue

Glue (15): Use a strong glue suitable for jewellery making, such as F6000.

BASIC TECHNIQUES

Once you have fused your design, it's ready to turn into a finished creation. There are just a few basic techniques to learn in order to make the projects in this book.

Using jump rings

1 *To open:* Grip each side of the ring with a pair of pliers and twist away from you.

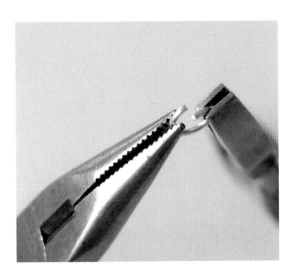

2 *To close:* twist back towards you so that the ends meet. Take care not to pull the rings apart sideways, as this will distort them.

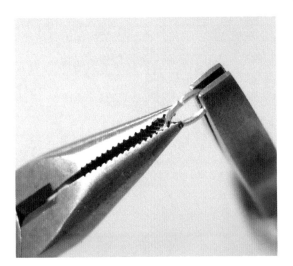

Bending

When the beads have been ironed and are still warm, it's possible to gently bend the design into a shape. Allow it to cool so that it retains that form.

1 After ironing, remove the ironing paper and carefully pick up the design – it will still be very hot. Protect your hands, if necessary, by using tweezers or a cloth.

2 Depending on the project instructions, either lay the design over a suitably shaped object (making sure it is heatproof, such as glass), or hold the design in the desired position and allow to cool completely.

TIP

If you are not completely happy with the shape achieved when bending your design, simply reheat it by ironing gently and start again.

Peyote stitch

Peyote stitch is one of the simplest bead weaving techniques and ideal to use with fuse beads. The first couple of rows need a bit of concentration, but then it's easy to master. The projects in this book use even count peyote, as they have an even number of rows.

1 Cut a suitable length of thread that you're happy to work with – a shorter thread may be easier to work with, but you will need to add new thread more frequently. About 10cm (4in) from the end, add a stop bead by going through the bead twice. This bead won't be part of your pattern, but is important as it stops your beads from sliding off the thread. It will be removed when you're finished, so it helps to use a contrasting colour bead for easy recognition.

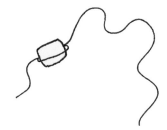

2 Using a darning needle, thread the number of beads required for your chart, following the pattern (see Reading a peyote stitch chart). This will make the first and second row of your weaving.

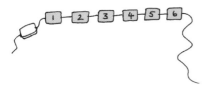

3 To work the next row, pick up another bead, miss out the lead bead you threaded and go back through the next one. It helps to hold the row of beads to keep them in place as you pull the thread through.

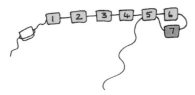

4 Pick up another bead following your pattern. Now skip over one bead and go through the following bead, pulling up until the bead lies neatly in place. Keep adding beads in the same way, skipping over one bead and through the next until you get to the end of the row.

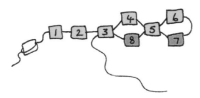

5 That's the tricky part over, so now you just need to fill in the gaps. Add a new bead for the top of the row, going through the bead that is sticking out. Each time you add the bead needed to fill the gap (following the pattern on the chart) and take the thread through the bead that is sticking out. As you work, make sure the beads are always pushed up firmly and the design is flat to keep a nice, even stitch. To add more thread as you go, simply cut a new length and tie a knot to join. The knot will be hidden away inside the beads.

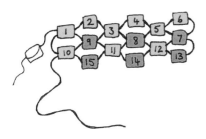

Reading a peyote stitch chart

Due to the way peyote stitch locks the beads together in an offset pattern, a little bit of care is required to follow a charted design. The first couple of rows are the hardest, so it helps to have these numbered to see the order of the beads.

The first line of beads you thread becomes both the first and second row of your design, in the example below you would pick up beads 1-6 in that order, alternating between orange and pink. You would then pick up bead 7, and work back through bead 5, pick up bead 8 and go through bead 3 and bead 9 through 1. The subsequent row you would pick up bead 10, work back through bead 9 and so on. Once these two rows are in place, it becomes easy to fill in the gaps by following the chart.

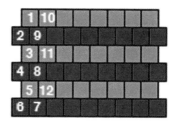

Joining peyote bands

Once you finish your peyote band, it will need joining to make a loop. This is done by interlocking the beads of the two ends and weaving the thread side to side through the joining beads to secure them together. Remove the stop bead from the other end of the band and tie the two ends together tightly with two knots. Snip the ends of thread.

TIP

Apply a small dab of strong, clear glue to the knot to keep it extra secure.

GEOMETRIC NECKLACE

You Will Need

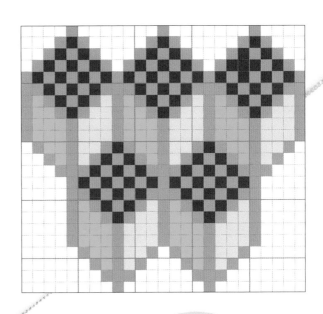

- Midi fuse beads (5mm)

- 45cm (18in) fine gold ready-made necklace

- Wire cutters

- Chain-nose/round-nose pliers

- Two 3mm gold jump rings

- Two 7mm gold jump rings

Making Up

1 Snip the centre link of the ready-made necklace and attach a small jump ring to each free end (see Using jump rings).

2 Attach a large jump ring to each small jump ring.

3 Attach each end of the necklace and jump rings to either side of the finished design, through the bead holes.

TIP

A fine chain looks great with this design, but make sure the links are big enough to allow the thickness of your jump rings.

THIRTIES FEATHER HAIRBAND

You Will Need

- Midi fuse beads (5mm)
- Black velvet hairband
- Needle and thread
- Strong glue

Making Up

1 Make and fuse one of each feather design. When ironed and still warm, gently bend to add a slight curve along the length each of feather (see Bending).

2 Position the smallest feather onto the hairband, just off centre and at a slight angle. Using a needle and thread, attach to the hairband, sewing through the first few beads.

3 Working down one side of the hairband, overlap the first feather with the medium one and sew onto the hairband in the same way as in step 2.

4 Repeat with the largest feather, securing firmly with several stitches.

5 Attach the circle gem design using glue to the base of the final feather, concealing the stitching.

TIP

For a different look, why not add a gem, pearl or button instead of the circle of fuse beads? This will add to the vintage feel.

MONOCHROME FRAME

You Will Need

- Midi fuse beads (5mm)

- 15 x 20cm (6 x 8in) photo frame with flat surface

- Strong glue

Making Up

1 Fuse the beads on one side only, as this will give more flexiblity to the design, while allowing it to lie completely flat on the frame.

2 Apply strong glue to the surface of the frame, ensuring it is completely covered, and lie the beaded design on top with the fused side facing up. Press firmly and allow to dry completely.

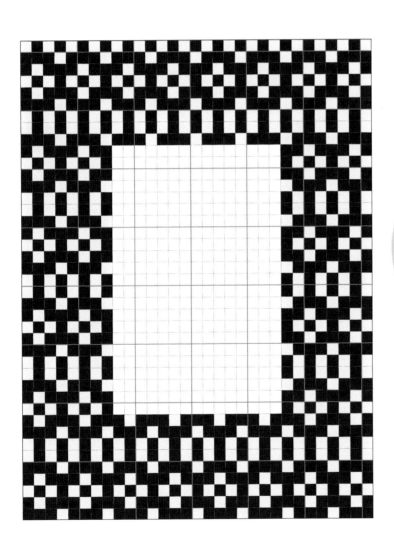

TIP

While gluing place a heavy object (such as a few books) on top of your frame to ensure the design has good contact with the glue and remains flat.

NAVAJO NECKLACE

You Will Need

- Midi fuse beads (5mm)

- 8m (8yd) brown beading thread

Making Up

1 Cut eight lengths of beading thread, each 1m (1yd) long.

2 Hold the lengths of thread together and tie a knot in the centre.

3 On each side, section the threads into two pairs of four, leaving four sections in total. Thread six turquoise beads through the four strands of each section.

4 On each side, group the eight threads back together and add three beads, alternating between yellow and brown. Do this on both sides of the necklace.

5 Divide the threads into pairs of four and repeat steps 3 and 4, six more times on both sides.

6 For the bottom part of the necklace, follow the diagram to bring the two sides together, splitting the threads and adding beads as shown.

7 To secure the final beads, tie two or three knots in each pair of threads, making sure the last bead can't slip over the knot. Cut the end to leave a tassel of around 2.5cm (1in).

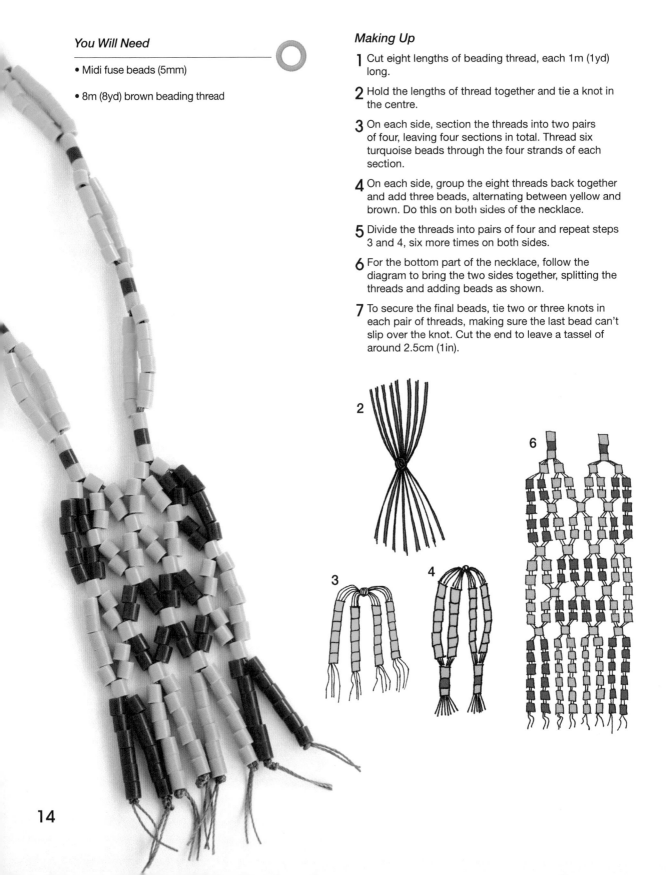

14

DRAGONFLY STICK PIN BROOCH

You Will Need

- Mini fuse beads (2.5mm)

- Stick pin blank

- Strong glue

Making Up

1 Iron the beads and while still warm, bend the wings up and hold in position until cool/set (see Bending).

2 Using strong glue, stick the pin brooch blank to the underneath of the finished design.

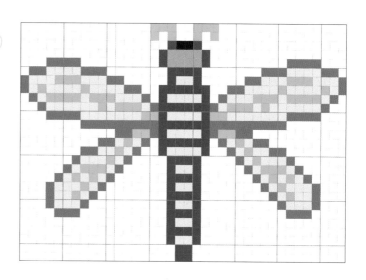

TIP

Alternatively, if you don't have a stick pin blank, you can use an ordinary brooch back.

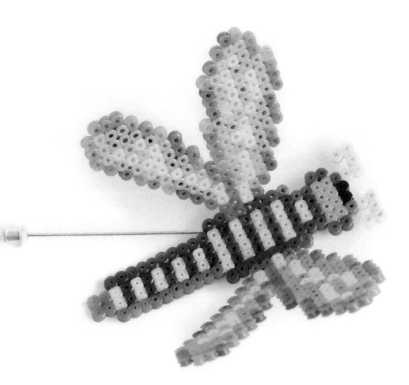

PSYCHEDELIC OWL BROOCH

You Will Need

• Mini fuse beads (2.5mm)

• Brooch back blank

• Strong glue

Making Up

1 Glue a brooch back blank to the back of the finished design.

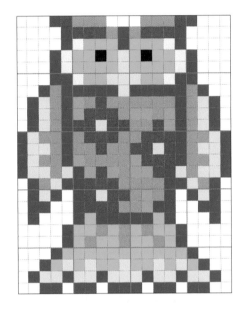

TIP

If you want a more realistic or different looking owl, use the same design, but with a brown and white colourway.

SWOOPING SWALLOW RING

You Will Need

• Mini fuse beads (2.5mm)

• Ring blank

• Strong glue

Making Up

1 Using strong glue, stick the ring blank to the back of the finished design.

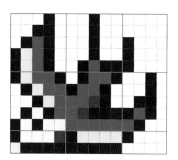

TIP

Make the same design in Midi fuse beads (5mm) for a matching brooch.

NARROWBOAT FLOWER POT

You Will Need

- Midi fuse beads (5mm)

- Terracotta flower pot (approx. 13cm/5¼in diameter, 12.5cm/5in tall)

- Large sheet of paper (approx. A3)

- Elastic bands

- Strong glue

Making Up

1 Wrap a sheet of paper around the flower pot, pressing it firmly around the rim and bottom to mark out an arc-shaped template. Remove and cut around the indentation to make a paper template.

2 Place the template onto the pegboard and create an outline of it on the board using with fuse beads. Try to keep the shape as smooth as possible.

3 Create the flower design in the centre of the beaded outline by using the chart. Fill in the remaining areas with dark green beads.

4 Iron the design on one side only, and while still warm, wrap the design around the flowerpot. Hold in place with elastic bands while cooling. Check the design fits neatly. If not, it's still possible at this stage to add more beads if necessary.

5 Measure the circumference of the pot rim. Using the chart to repeat the pattern, extend this beaded band to the required length to fit around the rim. If this band needs to be deeper than the chart for the pot you have, add rows of beads equally to the top and bottom.

6 Iron the red band on one side only and allow to cool.

7 Glue the base around the pot and the red beaded band around the rim, securing them in place with elastic bands as the glue dries.

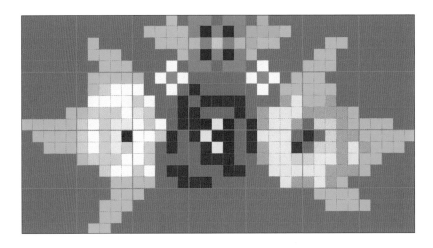

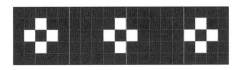

FOLK HEART RING

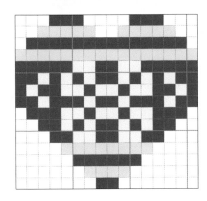

You Will Need

- Mini fuse beads (2.5mm)

- Ring blank

- Strong glue

Making Up

1 Using strong glue, stick the ring blank to the back of the finished design.

TIP

Make the same design in Midi fuse beads (5mm) for a matching brooch.

GROOVY GIFT TAGS

You Will Need

- Mini fuse beads (2.5mm)

- Thin white card

- Glue

- 22cm (9in) ribbon

- Thin white card

Making Up

1 Cut a 4 x 3.5cm (1½ x 1¼in) rectangle of card and glue to one side of your tags.

2 Fold the ribbon in half and pass the centre through the hole in the tag, creating a loop. Pass the ends of the ribbon through the loop and pull down to secure.

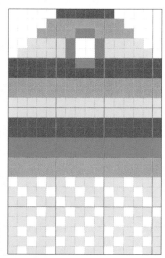
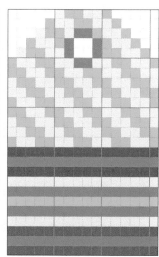

TIP

Come up with your own colour combinations for different occasions. For example red, green and white for Christmas, or pale pinks and blues for new baby gifts.

TRIBAL CUFF BRACELET

You Will Need

- Midi fuse beads (5mm)

- 0.5mm thick stretch elastic thread

- Darning needle

Making Up

1 Using peyote stitch (see Peyote stitch) thread the beads onto the stretch elastic thread following the chart.

2 Join the ends of the bracelet together by weaving the thread through the final beads and tie the two ends together securely.

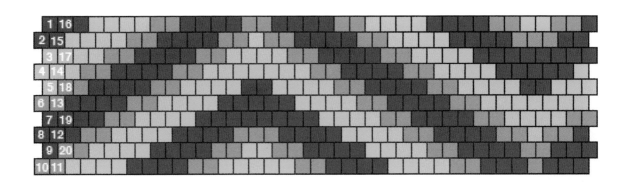

EGYPTIAN WING EARRINGS

You Will Need

• Mini fuse beads (2.5mm)

• Wire cutters

• Six 4.5mm gold jump rings

• 5cm (2in) fine gold chain

• Chain-nose/round-nose pliers

• Two gold hook earring wires

Making Up

1 Make two wing designs, following the chart.

2 Cut two pieces of chain, each 1cm (¼in) long, and attach one end of each chain to the top two corners of the design using jump rings (see Using jump rings).

3 Join the chains together at the top with another jump ring, adding the earring wire.

4 Repeat steps 2 and 3 for the other earring, making sure to flip the design over when attaching the earring wire to make a pair.

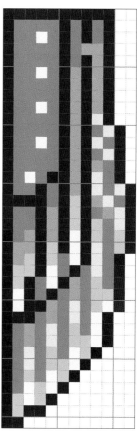

FAIR ISLE PEN HOLDER

You Will Need

• Midi fuse beads (5mm)

• 0.5mm thick stretch elastic thread

• Darning needle

• A clean, tin can without a serrated edge
(approx. 7cm/2¾in diameter, 10.5cm/4¼in tall)

Making Up

1 Using peyote stitch (see Peyote stitch), follow the chart and join the two ends of the band together by weaving through the joining beads.

2 The stretch elastic will allow the design to be stretched and placed over the tin to finish.

TIP

The beaded band can be glued to the tin to keep it secure and prevent it slipping around.

CHERRY DROP EARRINGS

You Will Need

- Mini fuse beads (2.5mm)

- 9cm (3½in) green chain (4 x 3mm links)

- Wire cutters

- Four 5mm green jump rings

- Chain-nose/round-nose pliers

- Two gold hook earring wires

Making Up

1 Make two cherry and leaf designs, following the chart.

2 Cut a length of chain 4.5cm (2in) long. Use a jump ring to attach this length of chain to the top of the cherry, through the hole in the design (see Using jump rings).

3 Place a jump ring through the final dark green bead in the leaf and use to attach to the other end of the chain and the earring wire.

4 Repeat steps 2 and 3 for the other earring.

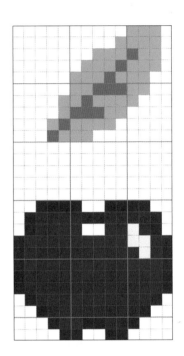

TIP

If you don't have any green chain, add a stalk using fuse beads instead to join the cherry and the leaf.

DAISY CHAIN NECKLACE

You Will Need

- Midi fuse beads (5mm)

- Thirty 6mm silver jump rings

- Chain-nose/round-nose pliers

- Eighteen 3mm silver jump rings

- 13cm (5in) fine silver chain

- Silver lobster clasp

Making Up

1 Make three large, four medium and eight small flowers. Iron the beads and while still warm, bend the petals up as desired and hold in position until cool/set (see Bending).

2 Attach a large jump ring to two sides of the large flowers, through the top corner bead (the last bead in the outside row of four). Link these flowers together using a small jump ring between each large jump ring (see Using jump rings).

3 Add two medium flowers to each side of the larger flowers in the same way.

4 Add four of the smallest flowers to each side of the necklace, using large jump rings through two opposite points on the sides of the flower and small jump rings to link.

5 Use a small jump ring to attach a length of chain 6.5cm (2½in) long to the final small flower on each side of the necklace.

6 Finish by adding another small jump ring to the top of each chain, plus a lobster clasp to one side.

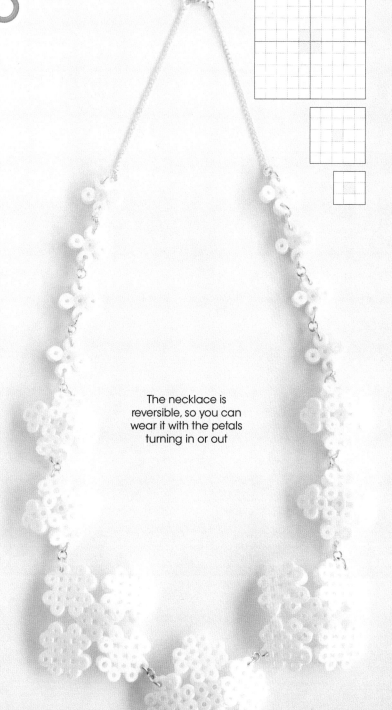

The necklace is reversible, so you can wear it with the petals turning in or out

GEOMETRIC CLOCK

You Will Need

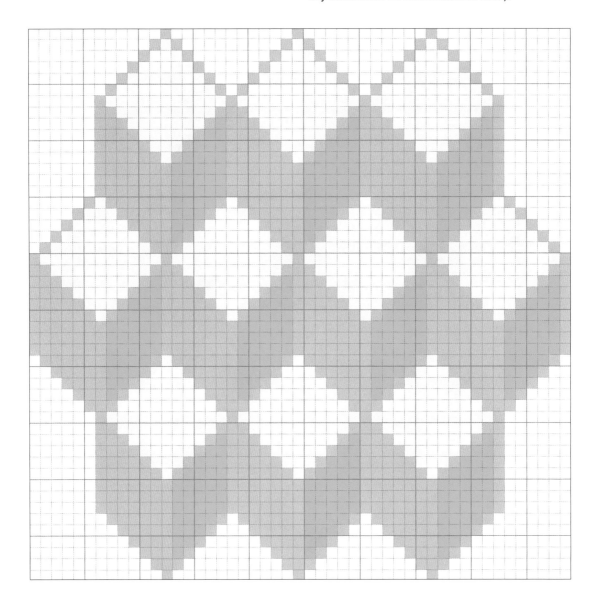

- Midi fuse beads (5mm)

- Clock mechanism (with 5–6cm/2–2½in hands)

Making Up

1 Check the clock mechanism shaft to see the size of the hole needed in the design. Leave out an appropriate number of beads in the centre.

2 When the design has been created and fused, place the mechanism through the hole, screw down the retaining nut and attach the hands (while at the same time referring to any instructions for the mechanism itself).

TIP

To get a good snug fit for the clock mechanism, it helps to round off the hole in the centre of the clock with a craft knife.

NAUTICAL HAIR CLIPS

You Will Need

• Mini fuse beads (2.5mm)

• Two metal hair clip blanks

• Strong glue

Making Up

1 Using strong glue, stick a hair clip blank to the back of each finished design.

TIP

For a larger design that would be perfect for a set of nautical coasters, use Midi fuse beads (5mm) beads with the same chart.

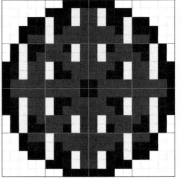

KITTY COMPACT MIRROR

You Will Need

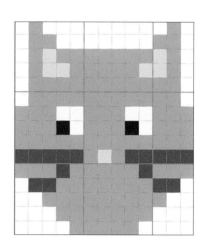

- Midi fuse beads (5mm)

- Plain compact mirror (6cm/3½in diameter)

- Pink ribbon bow

- Strong glue

Making Up

1 Using strong glue, attach the finished design to the top of the plain compact mirror.

2 Glue the ribbon bow at an angle on to the ear.

TIP

If you don't have a ready-made ribbon bow, simply use a short length of ribbon by folding the ends into the centre and stitch using a few running stitches. Pull up the thread to gather the bow and secure with a further few stitches.

PRETTY PASTEL DOILIES

You Will Need

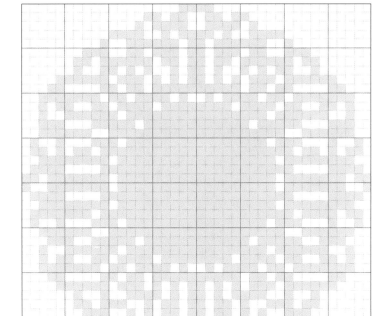

- Midi fuse beads (5mm)

TIP

Be very careful when ironing the doilies – some of the beads only touch by one corner, so check each bead is well fused before removing from the pegboard.

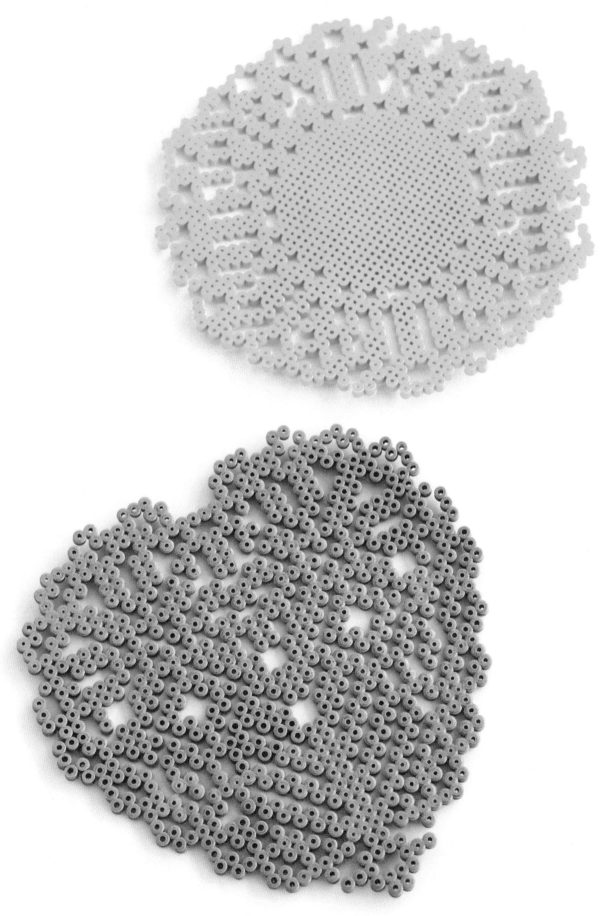

DOGGY BAG CHARMS

You Will Need

• Mini fuse beads (2.5mm)

• Bag charm blank

• Two 6mm silver jump rings

• Chain-nose/round-nose pliers

Making Up

1 Attach each dog design to the bag charm blank using a jump ring through one of the beads (see Using jump rings).

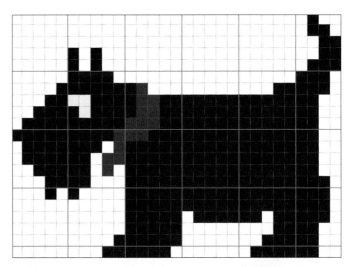

TIP

If you don't have a bag charm blank, use a keyring and two lengths of chain as an alternative.

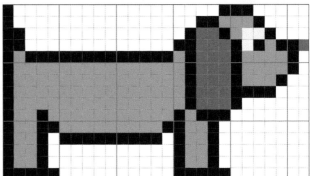

HOME SWEET HOME KEYRING

You Will Need

- Mini fuse beads (2.5mm)

- Keyring blank

- Chain-nose/round-nose pliers

Making Up

1 Attach the keyring blank to the roof of the house, using the gap in the design.

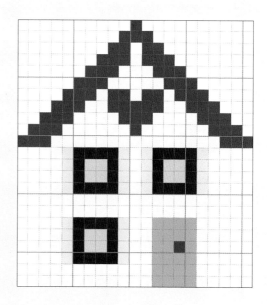

TIP

Personalize the colours and arrangement of the door and windows to match your own home.

BEACH HUT PICTURE

You Will Need

• Midi fuse beads (5mm)

• Strong glue

• A4 white card

• A4 white picture frame

Making Up

1 Iron the beads on one side only, so they lie evenly.

2 Glue the beach hut designs onto the card, fused side up. Carefully line them up.

3 Place the finished picture in the frame.

TIP

For a normal frame, you will not need the glass. If you'd like to protect your finished picture behind glass, use a box frame instead.

BUTTERFLY GARLAND

You Will Need

- Midi fuse beads (5mm)

- Pink embroidery thread (length as desired)

Making Up

1 Make several butterflies in different colours. The number of designs required will depend on how long you want your garland to be.

2 To join the butterflies, tie a 20cm (8in) length of embroidery thread to the bottom centre bead of a butterfly. String four to five loose fuse beads onto the thread at equal intervals by passing the thread through the bead twice to secure them in place.

3 Tie the other end of the thread to the top centre bead of the next butterfly. Continue in this way until you reach the desired length for your garland.

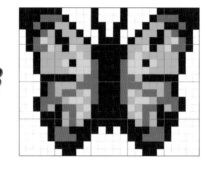

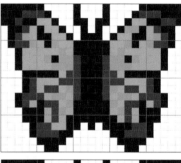

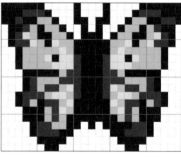

TIP

For a different look, add some dimension to your butterflies by bending gently while still warm to create formed wings.

FOXY BRACELET

You Will Need

- Midi fuse beads (5mm)

- Glass tumbler or jar

- String

- Three 6mm (¼in) silver jump rings

- Silver lobster clasp

Making Up

1 Iron the beads and while they're still warm, wrap around a glass tumbler or jar and tie with string. Remove when the beads have cooled(see Bending).

2 Attach a jump ring to the last black bead on the fox's nose, then attach another jump ring to this one (see Using jump rings).

3 Attach a lobster clasp to the last white bead on the tail using a third jump ring.

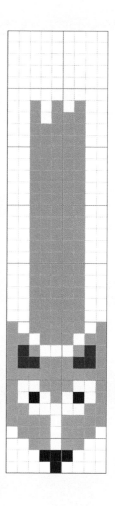

SCANDI TREE DECORATIONS

You Will Need

- Midi fuse beads (5mm)

- Red and white embroidery thread

- Darning needle

- 0.6cm x 12cm (¼in x 5in) red ribbon

Making Up

1. On the heart and star designs, after ironing add another bead to the centre top of each design, by fusing once more without using the peg board. This allows a bead to be added in the centre for hanging.

2. Using embroidery thread, stitch the designs onto the decorations by following the charts.

3. Fold the ribbon in half and pass the folded end through the top bead of the decoration to create a loop. Pass the ends of the ribbon through the loop and pull up. Tie the loose ends together in a secure knot.

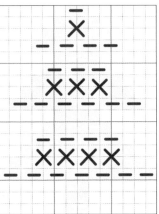

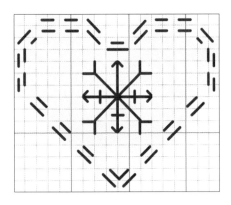

TIP

When ironing, ensure you leave a good-size hole in the top bead of each design, as this will be used to thread the ribbon onto the decoration.

FRUITY GLASS CHARMS

You Will Need

- Mini fuse beads (2.5mm)

- Six glass charm blanks

Making Up

1. Attach a glass charm blank through one of the top beads on each design.

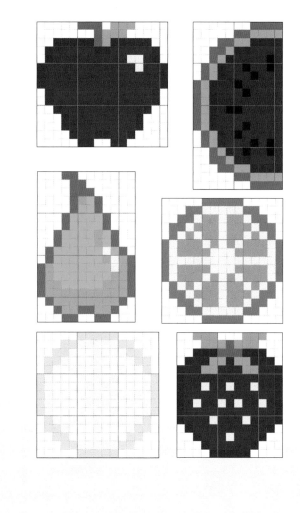

GRANNY SQUARE MUG RUGS

You Will Need

• Midi fuse beads (5mm)

TIP
Remember! Fuse beads have a low melting point, so avoid placing very hot items on the coasters.

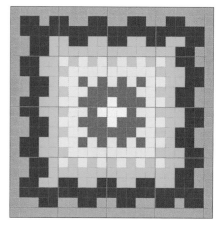

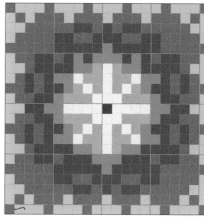

Change the colours used for a variety of effects.

BIRD AND BLOSSOM LAMP

You Will Need

- Midi fuse beads (5mm)

- Strong glue

- LED touch light

Making Up

1 Make up and fuse four of the bird design panels. Using the notches seen in the chart, interlock the panels to construct the walls of the cube. Glue each wall into place.

2 Make up and fuse one of the cloud designs, which will act as the top panel. Using the notches, glue into place on top of the cube.

3 Place the finished lamp over the LED touch light.

TIP

For a brighter light, make the lamp using translucent beads.

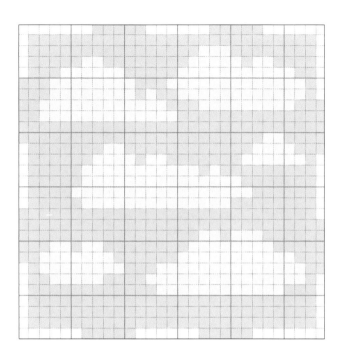

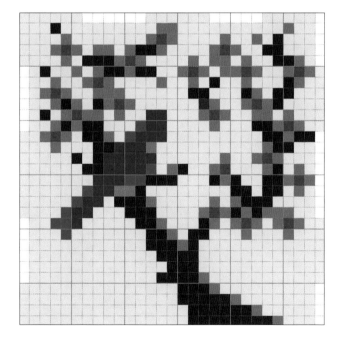

44

YUMMY FRIDGE MAGNETS

You Will Need

• Mini fuse beads (2.5mm)

• Six self-adhesive magnet squares

Making Up

1 Using the self-adhesive backing, attach the magnets to the back of each finished design.

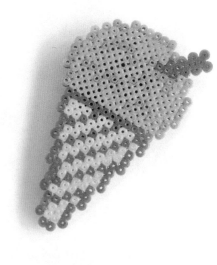

TIP

Use these designs to make brooches, hair clips, or whatever you fancy!

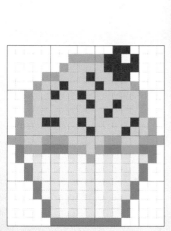
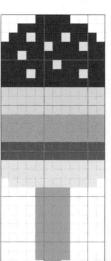
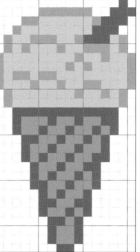
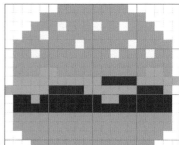

ACKNOWLEDGMENTS

Thank you to Ame, Jo and Charlotte at F&W Media International for bringing this book to life. Big thanks also to my family for letting fuse beads take over the whole house; I'm sure there are still some behind the sofa!

SUPPLIERS

Hama beads

craftycrocodiles.co.uk
Wide range of individual coloured beads.

hamabeads.com
Large selection of beads and pegboards. Worldwide delivery.

hobbycraft.co.uk
Good selection of beads and general crafting supplies.

Perler beads

amazon.co.uk
Mixed packs of beads.

eksuccessbrands.com
Perler brand website. International delivery.

Jewellery Findings

bluestreakbeads.co.uk
Coloured chain and jewellery findings.

dizzybeads.co.uk
For findings, ready-made necklaces and bracelets.

johnlewis.com
Good general jewellery making supplies.

ABOUT THE AUTHOR

Prudence Rogers can't remember a time when she wasn't drawing, painting, sewing or making something. She grew up in a highly creative family, so it felt natural for her to go on to study graphic design and begin her working career in print and design. She soon moved into the world of magazine publishing and became Art Director of *Devon Life* magazine. Book publishing was a natural progression and she has a long-standing career in the industry, covering all areas of design, art direction and illustration. It was not long before her love of making and crafting combined with her design skills led to her first book *The Unofficial Lego Jewellery Book*, which was published by David & Charles in 2014. She now works as a freelance graphic designer and illustrator from her home in Devon, UK.

A DAVID & CHARLES BOOK
© F&W Media International, Ltd 2014

David & Charles is an imprint of F&W Media International, Ltd
Brunel House, Forde Close, Newton Abbot, TQ12 4PU, UK

F&W Media International, Ltd is a subsidiary of F+W Media, Inc
10151 Carver Road, Suite #200, Blue Ash, OH 45242, USA

© F&W Media International, Ltd 2014

First published in the UK and USA in 2014

ISBN-13: 978-1-4463-0577-5 UK edition paperback
ISBN-10: 1-4463-0577-5 UK edition paperback

ISBN-13: 978-1-4463-0578-2 US edition paperback
ISBN-10: 1-4463-0578-3 US edition paperback

ISBN-13: 978-1-4463-7096-4 UK edition PDF ebook
ISBN-10: 1-4463-7096-8 UK edition PDF ebook

ISBN-13: 978-1-4463-7098-8 US edition PDF ebook
ISBN-10: 1-4463-7098-4 US edition PDF ebook

ISBN-13: 978-1-4463-7095-7 UK edition epub
ISBN-10: 1-4463-7095-X UK edition epub

ISBN-13: 978-1-4463-7097-1 US edition epub
ISBN-10: 1-4463-7097-6 US edition epub

Project Designer: Prudence Rogers
Content Director: Ame Verso
Desk Editor: Charlotte Andrew
Art Editor: Jodie Lystor
Photographer: Jack Kirby
Production Manager: Beverley Richardson

F+W Media publishes high-quality books on a wide range of subjects.
For more great book ideas visit: www.stitchcraftcreate.co.uk

Layout of the digital edition of this book may vary depending on reader hardware and display settings.

Printed in Great Britain
by Amazon.co.uk, Ltd.,
Marston Gate.